Eliciting Effective Interviews and Interrogations

An ISS Course Guide

By Steven Varnell

SCV Publishing, Apollo Beach Florida

For information about special discounts for bulk purchases, please contact Steven Varnell at isspartner@gmail.com

ISBN   978-0-9853821-6-2

ISBN   0-9853821-6-3

Other Titles by Steven Varnell

Criminal Interdiction
Tactical Survival
Behavior Analysis and Interviewing Techniques
Statement Analysis – An ISS Workbook
The Complete Interdiction and Survival Strategies

The development of this book is to assist anyone interested in the I&I process. I use the book as a part of my Eliciting Effective Interviews and Interrogations class. As such, it is not a sit down read but a guide through the process. It is an accumulation of technics from psychiatry to polygraph to skill set trained interrogation experts to employment personnel. The format is the culmination of decades of experience, research, interviews of experts in the various arts, training, and creativity. Its intention is to assist attendees of my lectures on the topic. The information is vast and requires experience to fully grasp all of the procedures. Therefore, use it as a guide going forward in our search for the actual purpose of the process, the truth.

Steven Varnell
Apollo Beach, Florida
2017

Understand that though the format I present is extensive, it is not intended as a step-by-step guide. The investigation, evidence, and the subject themselves will determine the location in the process to begin. A thorough pre-interview and interview will show you the way.

There is a myriad of potential possibilities in any interview. You have to be prepared to respond appropriately to the behavior presented by the subject.

For instance, you sit down to interview a subject in a theft case. The status of the subject is not yet determined. They may be a witness, an uninvolved employee or the perpetrator. Initially you may be prepared to conduct a full interview to determine the subject's involvement. You introduce yourself and the person starts crying.

You recognize this and move to the transitional interrogation (Explained later) without any intervening steps. Suppose the same person made a small admission, apologizing for the missing money. Again, you would respond to the interrogation phase. After the confession, return to the beginning of their account to learn the entire story.

In yet another scenario, after you explain the purpose of the interview the subject starts making excuses for the crime. You can now move the process forward agreeing with the subject. Empathy always follows admissions.

There are numerous opinions as to the number of steps that exist in an interview. The most common idea is that an I&I process consist of 5 steps:

Introduction
Rapport
Interview
Interrogation
Closure

In my opinion, the criminal interrogation consists of seven major phases and each is important for you to spend as much time as possible with:

Case Analysis
Introduction
Background Information
Interviewing
Transitioning to Interrogation
The Accusatory Phase
The Closure

Understanding the content of a narrative and the areas of interest to watch for, we initiate an interview with the person(s). Our objective is to start with what you know, determine what you do not know, and then shape your questions accordingly.

Before starting, understand that you may only get one opportunity to interview people.
Thoroughly complete your prep work or the Case Analysis before the interview. Examine their upbringing, religious, morals, topics of importance, how central their family is to them, importance of their reputation with friends etc.

Case Analysis

Every I&I begins with a thorough Case Analysis.
A study of the case file/witness interviews can indicate:
The probability of guilt
A possible motive
The personality structure of the subject
The probative value of the evidence in the case

If the evidence is irrefutable then this type of evidence gives the investigator confidence that he doesn't have if the evidence is subjective as with witness identification. We learn through experience that the toughest cases are those where the evidence is circumstantial in nature. The guilty person can create a plausible argument around the circumstantial evidence.

Case Analysis will sometimes indicate whether or not the suspect is involved in other crimes even from surrounding jurisdictions.
Case Analysis will suggest the existence of a mitigating factor which could be used later to help the suspect rationalize his act and make him more prone to tell the truth.
Case Analysis will suggest whether or not to ask "bait questions."

The first major decision you make in any interrogation session is whether to begin with an Accusatory or Non-Accusatory Interrogation.
Case Analysis will dictate your choice. Normally you begin with Non-Accusatory Interrogation.

Where guilt is obvious, you may want to begin with an Accusatory Interrogation by pointing out all of the evidence indicating the suspect's guilt.
This is the only time you break with normal procedure

There are several reasons for launching into an Accusatory Interrogation:
- It can create resignation in the suspect, wherein he is more apt to "give in" because he realizes he just can't lie around all the evidence.
- The forceful approach is psychologically devastating to the suspect because he realizes the futility of attempting to change your mind.
- By repeatedly hearing the evidence against him stated, the suspect realizes that he will be convicted even if he doesn't confess.
- This triggers the self-interest factor, wherein the suspect believes that if he is cooperative and tells the truth, he is going to get a lesser penalty.
- The whole idea of immediate Accusatory Interrogation is to point out that there is no question as to his guilt.
- There is only the question as to whether or not he has the fortitude to tell the truth.
- When you have a lot of evidence, you do not need any imagination so all you have to do is to keep restating the evidence you have.

It is more difficult when you do not know the truth and their guilt or innocence is not obvious. When this happens then subjective analysis is required.

Subjective analysis becomes an art form dependent upon perceptive questioning.

A procedure is necessary for the subjective analysis. This procedure will enable you to form a more definitive opinion and assist in the later interrogation.

Do a complete case analyses because it is impossible to efficiently complete any task unless you know what you are trying to accomplish.

This is accomplished by first identifying the elements of the crime to be proven and then determine the unknown details.

Determine why you need to interview the subject. Once you know the probable relationship to the crime, you are in a position to judge the details they should have.

Therefore, you should write down the unknown points in the form of questions arranged in a logical order. Usually, during the topic of the unknowns, you will need to ask a number of questions to resolve the questions.

At 8:30 am on Christmas morning, someone entered the office of your former employer and stole $27,000.00.

The crime scene evidence tells us there was not a forced entry, the alarm was activated the afternoon before, and the money was locked in the safe in the owner's office. Nothing was relocked after the theft.

We need to know:
The events of your morning.
Alibi.
Why he left job?
Did he leave his house on Christmas morning?
Was he ever given an office key?
Did he turn in his office key?

Was he ever aware of the alarm code?
Did he ever have to go into the office safe?
Was he provided the code to the safe?

If there are multiple people, interview the least likely suspect or probable witnesses first and continue in order of importance.
This way we will have all of the statements before sitting with our prime suspect.

<u>Preparing the Interview Room</u>

Room set up and sweep, audio-video, the case analysis results, possible evidence themes, bait questions, water, and have at least 6 prepared broad questions to expand knowledge rapidly.
Have a simple signal for others so as not to interrupt the interview at a critical point.

Do not allow a subject to drink anything with caffeine because It will reduce the effects of fatigue as much as 4%.
Before entering the room, offer a restroom break.
Confirm that the witness/suspect has been thoroughly searched.

INTRODUCTION

Introduce yourself and present you credentials.
Many agencies but not all have this step as a regulation. This starts to confirm your authority in the room.
Smile and shake their hand if possible.
If there are others present, introduce professionally.
Ask them to identify themselves.

When we are down, we turn to our friends for support. This is why they must see you as someone they can talk to with comfort.

Most inexperienced investigators do not realize the importance of the introduction.
The first 5-20 seconds is a person's first impression.
Negative first impressions are hard to overcome.
Look, act, dress, and use language of respect.

Symbolic communication is the message we send through inanimate objects and we are always giving out a continuous stream of signals about ourselves. Your appearance is part of a reciprocal interaction and that, psychologically, the degree to which we are willing to accept what another person has to say depends on three things:
< How trustworthy the person is seen to be
< How qualified the person is seen to be
< What type of person the individual is seen to be

What you communicate symbolically deserves your conscious attention.
We say a great deal about ourselves through our posture, appearance, grooming, style of dress, body language, and vocal tone.
A poor opening can contaminate the process before it has had a chance to start.

Purpose Confirmation

Almost everyone experiences apprehension when the meaning of a law enforcement interview is not clear; therefore, address the issue early.
Make a clear statement of purpose. The statement of purpose is not meant to reveal detailed facts of

the case but rather, to provide an overview of what is to come--inquiries pertaining to a specific investigation.

A well-stated purpose will provide a reason for the interviewee to talk with you.

Phrasing the Introduction - "John, as you know, we are conducting an investigation into these allegations made by ... . The purpose of our investigation is to determine the truth about what happened. The purpose of this interview is so we can take your statement and get your information about this. I appreciate your cooperation in this matter and I'm sure you're just as eager to get to the truth of this as we are. It is imperative that you are 100% truthful with me. The truth is like being pregnant; you either are or are not. There is no middle or gray area. Together, we can get past almost anything, but we cannot get past a lie. You must tell only the truth. Do you understand?"

Confirm they have no appointments in the next few hours otherwise reschedule.

Warn them of any embarrassing questions based on the type of investigation.

Conduct a physical/mental assessment.

Physical/Mental Assessment

To initiate the process it can be important to show the subject was fully understanding of the interview

What is your general health?...Excellent, good, fair or poor...Explain.

Have you taken any medication in the past 24 hours?...

Ask about effects of medication...You may have to go to PDR or internet.
Alcohol in the past 24hrs?
Are you presently being treated by a doctor?...Explain...
Pregnancy?
Amount of sleep in past 24 hours? What is the norm?

Tell them you are committed to obtaining a detailed statement and they must include every aspect.
After the introduction, allow the suspect to give a brief synopsis of the story.
Partway through, cut him off. You now have some insight into what position the suspect is going to take. His brief story provides a format for your questions.

After you have stopped the suspect, tell him that he will have plenty of time to talk, but that you have a procedure to follow. State that you want to get some general background information before discussing his story in detail.
This statement does two things;
It puts you in immediate command of the interview and establishes dominance.

It frustrates a lying suspect with a rehearsed story because he did not immediately get to tell his script. The threat of having his story analyzed in detail creates anxiety in the suspect and his defensiveness will become more apparent.

Background information

Initiate rapport/baseline/relaxation building with generalized questions.
This is a non-accusatory phase interview where you can ask, "Tell me about yourself," how their day was progressing, traffic, etc.
Attitude questions help start the interview correctly.
How are you this morning?
Do you like sports?

At this point, obtain the subject's general background information.
This provides a brief sketch of the suspect.
There is an old saying, "When you know a person's past, you know their future."

At the beginning of the interview, you do not go into detail about what you're there for.
If they keep asking questions about why they are there, they are nervous.
There is no hurry. What you want to do is get the person talking and feeling good about talking to you.

Use the bio sheet to gather and confirm a correct past.
Ask if previously questioned but not arrested in another matter? (Where, What, When) This may reveal prior information from a different agency that you otherwise would have no knowledge.

Taking the biographical data accomplishes several things:
- You have something upon which to make a subjective analysis of the interviewee.

- You may see a basic propensity to commit the act in question.
- You can evaluate the suspect's degree of cooperation in answering questions.
- You will see the presence or absence of hostility and/or evasiveness and begin baselining him.
.

Thoroughness in this category of questioning eliminates potential embarrassment in court under cross-examination for failing to obtain pertinent information about the subject's background such as:
Psychological treatment
Substance abuse
Alcoholism
Illness

As you discuss his general background you provide an opportunity for the suspect to lie such as an arrest record, job dismissal, drug-use, or has he lied in a previous investigation.

You cannot be too thorough when taking a person's general background.
Each category you cover is a potential gold mine of information for later use.
For example, in larceny cases, when you cover the suspect's financial obligations, motive sometimes becomes obvious as you discover expenses for which the suspect cannot explain the source of his funds.

You will use this information later to try to trick the suspect into admitting issues of the crime. You set up the bluff by telling the suspect that you conducted a background check on him before he came to your office. You then ask questions about issues as if you already know the answers.

When you discuss the suspect's job history, you set up a potential later argument by asking the suspect if he has ever been fired for stealing, accused of stealing on a job, or questioned about stealing.

You can later tell him that you conducted a thorough background check on him and that he did not tell the whole truth about one of the issues.
This bluff hardly ever backfires.
The odds are that even if the suspect is innocent of any wrongdoing on a previous job, if he worked handling money or small merchandise, he probably has been questioned about losses.

If the suspect admits that he was accused of stealing or questioned about it, this admission can be used to obtain a confession in the case or that he is the common denominator in different thefts on different jobs.

Be careful with sales people, because a lot of them lie for a living.
They are generally extroverts and very articulate.
They love selling themselves and trying to deceive investigators.

When you question a suspect about any personal problems such as divorce, separation, illness, losses, etc., you set up one of the best arguments:
"It wasn't your character that caused you to (steal, drink, use drugs, commit robbery, assault, batter, etc.) it was your personal problems."

When you question a suspect about an arrest record, you have a credibility test.
"Were you guilty of the crime?"
"Did you plead guilty?"
"Did you confess to the crime?"

If the suspect always protests his innocence despite numerous arrests, it is obvious that you have a anti-social, anti-authority person who projects guilt on society and hardly ever makes an admission against self-interest.
You may not get a confession, but at least you know whom you are dealing with.

In fraud/arson cases, you generally only get one shot at the suspect, so you have to be thorough in your questioning to establish possible motive. Ask background questions such as:
"Has your business been up for sale?"
"Are you behind in your mortgage or rent payments?"
"Have you ever filed for bankruptcy?"
"Have you ever been sued by any creditor?"
"Have you made any prior insurance claims?"
"Have you recently increased your insurance coverage?"
"Do you have Business Interruption Insurance?"
"Did you remove any official records from your office prior to the fire?"
"Did you remove any personal items from your office prior to the fire?"
"Did you order any repair work on any appliance or machine in your building prior to the fire?"
"When was the last time you purchased any accelerant such as gasoline, kerosene, etc.?"

"Did you move a large amount of merchandise in or out of your building during the several days prior to the fire?"

When you question suspects about their general educational background, don't assume because they only have a 6th grade education, that they are stupid.
They could have a Ph.D. in "street smarts."
Remember, the liar is the smartest person in the room because he knows the truth and you don't.

While taking the general background information, make an initial assessment as to whether or not the suspect is tough-minded enough to have committed the act in question. These people generally radiate arrogance.

When discussing a suspect's personal habits, such as his alcohol or illegal drug use, look for his use of the defense mechanism of disassociation to respond to normal life difficulties. The continuing practice of self-deception makes him very convincing when lying to others.

With a viable suspect and the motive is not obvious, it is often because you did not dig deeply enough into the suspect's background.
Sometimes, even when you know the suspect is guilty, you are confused by why he committed the crime. Many times, there just isn't any obvious reason.

I have learned through experience in criminal cases, "That something never comes from nothing."
There is always a catalyst; a real or imagined

grievance, a personality defect, or a history of abnormal behavior, which if known at the time of your interview, will make the suspect's motive obvious.

Always conduct a thorough background check into the suspect's life history.
After you have obtained the suspect's general background, you are ready to question the suspect regarding the specifics of the case.

Honesty Check

Ask, "Is it your intention today to be completely honest with me?"
If yes, praise. "Good I am glad to hear that you want to resolve this issue."
The subject is asked to assess his own level of honesty.
"How about you, John? In terms of honesty, how would you rate yourself personally on a scale of 1 – 100."

If estimate is not between 95 – 100 percent continue by saying, "Really? That's kind of low. Most people are higher than that. You know yourself better than I do—give me as accurate an assessment of your honesty as you can."

Another Honesty evaluation method:

As a part of the discussion, we want them to focus on "what is a lie?"
To begin with, ask the subject to give you their definition of a lie.

After they describe their definition of a lie, ask the subject, "Are you a liar?"

Again, the usual answer is "no."

Ask them "how many lies do you have to tell to be a liar?"

They may give you a number; however, you want them to recognize that if you tell one lie, you are a liar.

You can tell them that everyone is a liar.

Ask the subject "What is a lie?"

Tell them, "A lie is something that is not 100% truthful."

Write on a pad the number "99.9%" for the subject to see, point to it and ask them, "If an answer is 99.9% truthful, is it still a lie?"

Get them to agree it is a lie.

This focuses the subject on the act of lying, bringing it to the front of their mind.

Now that you've established the definition of a lie and the psychological set, ask the subject a question such as,

"Have you ever lied to anyone in authority?" or "Have you ever lied to supervisor about a policy violation?"

Everyone has done this in their past.

It is an old offense and currently is of no consequence.

The subject will usually lie and say they have not lied and can observe and establish how this person lies.

After they say this, you can even discuss how important it is to tell the truth or to describe why they just lied.

Explain how you know they have done this in the past, just as everyone else has — even you. When they agree that they just lied, even though it is a minor lie, they have now admitted lying to you. This reinforces the psychological set that will generate the stress that drives the behavior. This is also a big step in building rapport for the person to admit they have lied to you.

As we begin our discussion and they start to lie, the thought of lying comes to their mind, creating anxiety. The anxiety creates the stress that generates the behavior we evaluate for that question.

Additional questions you can use to help establish the psychological set are:

1.)   Have you ever lied to someone you love and trust?
2.)   Have you ever lied to someone to make yourself look good?
3.)   Have you ever lied on an application to make yourself look good?
4.)   Have you ever lied on your taxes?
5.)   Have you ever lied to the police?
6.)   Have you ever lied to a teacher at school?
7.)   Have you ever lied to a person to break off a relationship?
8.)   Have you ever lied to your children to make them behave?
9.)   Have you ever lied to your parents or siblings to avoid a family event?
10.)   Have you ever lied to someone to get off the phone?

Other Options
"The investigation into this matter will be very thorough. How do you think it will turn out against you?"
"John we are asking everyone to give us their thoughts or opinions of this issue. Please give me five reasons why you think this happened."
A suspect will list either motives or contributing factors.

Non-Accusatory Interview

Have a prepared witness statement which is very thorough, real or contrived, to use as a demonstration as to what is expected from them. This gives them guidance.

Use the Witness Interview headings to assist in showing what is expected of them.
Explain the type of crimes you investigate and include the current crime type in the middle. Softly offer their legal warnings at the point where your jurisdiction requires.
Take a break to confer with observers at any point deemed necessary.

Present every word with an even tone and pitch. Do not place any emphasis upon a single word in the questioning. Be direct and ask in a simple non-discreet manner, people are less likely to take offense.

Remember the 3 strikes rule – once you have asked a subject a question 3 times and have not received an appropriate answer, do not get aggressive. This only builds a wall.

Several factors affect Non-Accusatory Interviews:

THE ENVIRONMENT/LOCATION – Already discussed. The best place is in a prepared room.

PHYSICAL POSITIONING BETWEEN SUSPECT AND INTERROGATOR
Maintain the 5-7 feet social proxemics with nothing between you.

THE ATTITUDE OF THE INTERROGATOR
In my opinion, nothing affects questioning more than the attitude and behavior of an interrogator. Types of interrogators whose attitude and behavior prevent successful interrogation:
- The investigator who fears that the suspect will not confess and generally finds some excuse not to interrogate.
- The investigator who is reluctant to ask the hard questions, who lets the suspect do all the talking and who sits there like a human tape recorder. The danger of this behavior is that suspects construe the investigator's silence as a weakness and will not confess to someone they do not respect.
- The investigator who identifies with the suspect and wants to believe him.
- The investigator who is fearful of creating a bitter relationship with the suspect and will never say to the suspect, "You are lying."
- The investigator who becomes married to a particular theory, who loses objectivity and who is reluctant to change his mind even when confronted

with evidence that clearly refutes his theory. (Confirmation Bias)

- He assumes everyone is guilty so that he will not risk being fooled by a truly guilty person. This attitude or bias is responsible for most miscarriages of justice.

- The investigator who lacks imagination or doesn't know what to say to the suspect is the type that lets a lot of people off the hook.

Good interrogators know that they will not always get a confession.
It is however, necessary that they always take a detailed statement from the suspect.

The more detail he has to relate, the better your chances are for a definitive evaluation of what the subject has to say.
A single question requiring a simple "yes" or "no" answer provides you with little or no information upon which to base an analysis of truth or deception.

HOW MUCH TIME HAS THE SUSPECT HAD TO PREPARE HIS LIES?
A suspect knows the loopholes in his story and if given sufficient time, he will fabricate a persuasive lie.
He learns to simulate innocence by repeating a lie, which then replaces the memory of what actually occurred. (Memory Manipulation)

Now that you know some of the factors that can undermine questioning, I would like to suggest some general rules to follow when questioning suspects in all types of cases.

HOW TO QUESTION IN THE INTERVIEW PHASE

I believe that there are categories of questions that can be asked in all types of cases.
When a person has to describe his behavior and a sequence of events, smart questioning should reveal whether or not the person is lying.
The secret is to be thorough in the questioning. In essence, what you have to do is to go below the level of the suspect's defense by presenting him with questions that he did not anticipate.

The whole purpose of asking questions is to force one of two things to happen:
The guilty person will respond verbally in a nonsensical manner which makes his lies evident.
A behavioral response is elicited that makes guilt obvious; the subject becomes hostile, evasive, or non-responsive to the inquiry.

To question, you must have one or more theories about how the crime was committed in mind. The theories act as a framework and suggest potential questions to ask. The goal of your questioning is to prove or disprove a particular theory.

When that theory is no longer operative, you move to a new theory. You begin to formulate your theories based on Case Analysis.
Questioning takes imagination.
You have to imagine how the crime was committed. You cannot have theories without imagination.

When you question, you attempt to link the person to the crime by:

Evidence - How does the suspect explain the evidence against him?
Motive - Does it exist, and if so, is it strong enough to prompt the crime?
Character - Is there a basic predisposition to commit the act in question?
Opportunity to commit the act - What is the alibi?
Behavior - Was the suspect's behavior at the time of the crime indicative of guilt, or was it just coincidental?

TEN RULES TO FOLLOW WHILE QUESTIONING

Rule One
Always Question Chronologically
It allows the story to unfold before your mind's eye. You must project yourself into the scene and imagine the story unfolding before you as if you were watching a video tape.

As you see the story unfold, each sequence of events described by the suspect suggests the next potential question.
It enhances the memory recall of the innocent person. With the guilty, it allows you to judge what they emphasize and what they gloss over.

The guilty always emphasize the safe areas and avoid a detailed description of their behavior at the time of the crime.
Simply put, in which part of the story is the suspect comfortable?
Questioning chronologically pressures the guilty suspect by forcing him to create lies to unexpected questions.

The innocent suspect simply employs memory recall to answer the questions.
Astute questioning relaxes the innocent suspect because your thoroughness gives him confidence that you are going to establish the truth.

Rule Two
<u>The First Category of Questions Should Always pertain to the Catalyst</u>
What triggered the act?
Every overt act has a precursor condition.
It is your job to figure out what potentially could have motivated the act.
In this category of questions, you see the possible motivation for the act for the first time.

During this phase, formulate questions to obtain information to answer the following in your own mind:
Did anything abnormal happen?
Was there a break in the routine?
What was the suspect's mood at the time?
Were there any personal problems, arguments, etc.?
Was the suspect suffering from any emotional turmoil?
Was there use of alcohol or drugs?
Why was the suspect there, and what was the suspect doing?
Was the suspect's behavior abnormal in any way?
Was it different from past behavior?
Was the suspect the common denominator in similar instances?

Rule Three
Ask Memory Questions
Remember, fear contaminates memory. Constantly force the subject to be more explicit. Ask questions to ascertain if any incidental situations occurred that might lend credibility to the suspect's story.

Generally, when innocent people relate a story they relate an incidental situation that occurred around the time of the crime, but which has no connection to it.
If that incidental situation is later verified, it lends credibility to the suspect's story.
For example, "At the time of the shooting, a man was walking his dog, and he must have been deaf because he never turned around."

If there are voids in the suspect's story, do not fill in the voids to make his story more logical. Do not make any suggestions as to what you know did not occur, you will enhance his lies. The voids in the suspect's story can be used as a wedge in Accusatory Interrogation.

Rule Four
Ask Verification Questions
"Who witnessed the act?"
"Who shared the experience?"
"Who was the first person you told about what occurred?"
"What were your feelings at the time; anger, fear, bewilderment?"
"What was your reaction to the situation?"

Evaluate whether the suspect's emotions are normal for the situation. Were they what you would expect from others?

"Have you figured out what happened?"
"What do you think happened?"
Was normal curiosity satisfied? An innocent person will genuinely try to figure out what happened. By contrast, a guilty person doesn't have to, he already knows the truth.

Rule Five
Ask Questions That Test the Logic of the Story
Does the suspect's story conform to the laws of probability?
Did the suspect's behavior conform to what a normal person would have done in a similar situation?
Is the suspect's description of what occurred probable in light of the sequence of events stated?

Ask questions regarding alternative options.
"Why did you chose 'A' rather than 'B'?"
"Since you were not forced, why did you do anything at all?"

Be suspicious of a suspect who defends his actions too strongly when it is obvious that an alternative would have been better. The innocent will generally say, "Yeah, I guess you're right, I should have done something else."
Always ask why a person did something in each sequence of events. It is more difficult to lie about "why" he did something than about "what" he did.

Ask questions so that the suspect suggests possible explanations for what occurred.
Many times what a person does not say is more important than what the person does say. What he omits is probably the underlying basis for what actually occurred.
The guilty are reluctant to speculate about things that threaten them.

Rule Six
<u>Ask Questions to Determine the Nature of the Story</u>
Guilty people keep their story concise because by doing so there is less ground to defend.
Most people lead from strength.
When they tell a story, they feature the area where they are comfortable.

Ask questions to see if the suspect is featuring peripheral matters over what the suspect was actually doing at the time of the crime.
Guilty people answer questions in a superficial manner.
A good interviewer never accepts anything at face value and always explores a superficial answer to reveal that it lacks substance.

Ask questions to see if the suspect changes the story when confronted with contrary evidence. In most instances when a person lies about a part, they lie about the whole.
Innocent people as a rule, do not change their story because they know what actually happened, but can add additional information for clarity.

Guilty people will project guilt by "opening up the crime to the world" and making everybody a suspect.

Ask questions to see if the suspect offers unrealistic explanations for how the crime may have been committed.

Guilty people are also masters of exclusion.

Question them as to how far they will go to exclude themselves from any physical or mental connection to the crime.

Do they know who committed the act?

Do they suspect anyone?

Have they ever fantasized about a similar act?

Under what condition would they consider committing the act?

Have they heard or read about a similar act?

Guilty people will feign a lack of interest.

Be particularly suspicious of a person whose entire defense is reduced to a singular argument. For example, "I wouldn't steal the money because I can get all the money I want from my parents."

"I wouldn't burn my business because I was making money."

A singular statement designed to convince has to overcome by perceptive questioning. Failure to do so allows the suspect to continue lying protected by a statement which he believes is irrefutable.

Ask questions to determine what tactic the subject is employing to defend himself.

Does the person argue a specific innocence based on fact, or is the person attempting to exclude himself by alleging good character?

Ask questions to see if the suspect portrays realistic feelings and emotions regarding the questioning of the crime.

An unemotional demeanor is suspicious.

As a defense mechanism, guilty people put themselves in an emotional "neutral slot" to avoid any manifestations of guilt.

This type of suspect fails to express feelings and avoids the use of painful words.

Ask questions to determine the consistency of the suspect's story.

An investigator should be suspicious of a person who leaves out important details that were told to the others.

Did he leave them out because he does not want to repeat the lie to you?

Is there a logical explanation for the omission?

An investigator should be suspicious of a suspect who offers a last minute detail in an effort to convince. If something is important to the suspect's defense, it should have been mentioned up front.

Rule Seven
Ask Questions That Reveal the Defense
Mechanism of Projection.

Most guilty people project guilt.

They blame anyone but themselves.

They seek to justify the act by blaming others.

This is a common tactic employed by guilty people.

This particular phase of questioning can be revealing in the determination of truth.

If I was limited to the number of questions to render an opinion as to guilt or innocence, one would be,

"What is your theory about this crime?"
Innocent people are generally comfortable with any question because they are telling the truth.
Guilty people become nervous when asked about something they are trying to avoid or suppress.

For that reason, the suspect should be asked projective questions such as:
"Why is the accuser saying this about you?"
"Do you think that the witness is lying?"
"How do you think you would do on a polygraph test?"
"Do you think this is a real theft?"
"Do you think the accuser made up this story?"

Rule Eight
<u>When You Have Nothing to Evaluate, You Have to Force an Evaluation</u>
The most difficult subjects to interrogate are those that employ the tactic of repeated assertion.
They keep saying,
"I don't know anything about it."

The underlying philosophy of this subject is encompassed in the saying,
"It is easier to believe a lie heard a thousand times, than to hear the truth for the first time."
If a suspect says, "I don't know anything about it and you have little or no evidence to the contrary." the investigator asks himself, "What am I going to talk to this guy about?"
The answer is his alibi.

Questioning the suspect about where he was at the time of the crime allows you the best opportunity to assess their credibility.

Innocent people look and sound truthful when relating their alibi. They will appear confident because they know they are telling the truth. You have to ask penetrating questions to reveal the false alibi.

Guilty people fail to verify their alibi by independent witnesses or documentation.
They may employ over-kill in verification in an effort to convince you of their whereabouts at the time of the crime.
Evaluation of the alibi is one of the best methods for getting some idea as to probable guilt or innocence.

If the guilty suspect, in his argument, disconnects physically from the crime, he will also disconnect mentally. This affords you another opportunity to make an evaluation.

You have to ask yourself how comfortable the suspect is in talking about the crime.
The guilty will try to disassociate from the crime by not offering any theories, suspicions nor any desire to figure it out.
In contrast, the innocent, knowing they didn't commit the crime, have a normal curiosity as to who committed the act and how.

If the investigator gains the confidence of those interviewed, the best lie detectors are fellow employees. If your case involves multiple people from the same office, the innocent will enjoy supplying both theories and suspects. You cannot hide what you are from fellow employees eight hours a day, five days a week.

If a person is reluctant to discuss the crime in question, this generally means he has no need to theorize about the crime; he already knows the answer.

When you have no story to evaluate, evaluate the subject's alibi, and his defensiveness or lack thereof.

Rule Nine
<u>Ask Questions to Determine Post-Act Behavior</u>
When a person commits a crime, the person generally manifests the act by questionable post-act behavior.

We often see bizarre behavior on the part of the guilty.

Attempting suicide.

Checking into a hospital with a sudden illness.

Leaving town.

Quitting a job.

Getting drunk.

Contacting an attorney before being questioned or accused.

Setting up an alibi.

Tempting fate by some reckless behavior.

Doing something nice for somebody like bringing flowers to his wife or buying lunch for fellow employees with stolen money.

Changing a routine which has not varied in the past.

Question suspects about their activities during the several hours after the crime.

If any suspicious act is revealed, or any change in normal routine noted, you have to ask yourself the question:

"Did the crime prompt them to do that?"

The suspect has not prepared for the post events, only the crime itself and has no rehearsed answers.

Rule Ten
You Can't Think of Every Question You Should Ask
You will discover that many people will not simply
volunteer information because we did not ask the
specific questions.
Without the training and experience this problem
will continue.

You cannot think of everything, therefore conclude
your questioning with an all-encompassing question
like:
"Is there anything that you didn't tell me because I
didn't ask you the question?"
It is amazing the number of times you receive the
response, "Well, there is one thing ... "

People become defensive when they are asked too
many questions.
They reach their saturation point so ask as many
open ended questions until clarification is required.
Focus your questions with the interrogatories, who,
what, where, when, why, which, and how
Use TEDS-PIE and ask for the free narrative.

TEDS - PIE
Created by Dr. Edward Geiselman and the London
Metropolitan Police.
Another acronym to help you remember and to
allow variations to the questioning not as easily
recognized by the interviewee.
TEDS - PIE
TEDS stands for:
• "Tell me..."
• "Explain to me..."
• "Describe for me..."
• "Show me...."

PIE stands for:
- "Precisely..."
- "In detail..."
- "Exactly...."

Expect the first narrative to be very short.
Give them a narrative review so they hear how lacking their story is and repeat that you need everything.
If it is a shortened version, gather all of the information on the topic with continuators.
"What else" or "What happened next?"
This is so you can stay on topic and create clarifying questions.

Your approach has to be with questions that they are not prepared for.
The first question you will want to know is, "Did they commit the crime?" However, if you come straight out and ask, they can tell you their prepared answer of "no."

The more they say it, the more entrenched they become. They can prepare their script to anticipated questions. When you allow an obviously guilty person to debate, you give him hope. A suspect has to get the impression that you are not going to take "no" for an answer.
It is the interviewer's job to make sure that you ask questions in a manner which is easily understood. It is the interviewee's job to answer the questions.
Along this line, we must keep things simple.

After they complete the initial free recall, depending on the type of case, it can be divided into the before, during, and after phase.

Ask an open-ended question of "Tell me everything that happened from A-B." When satisfied ask about B-C and conclude with C-D.

This is a funneling style of questioning.
Start with the open-ended overall, open-ended specific, closed-ended for clarification, and adding BAI questions.

For a clear stimulus response, the questions should contain only one idea, keep it short, simple, and straight forward to prevent confusion as to which part to answer.
If the case involves a burglary, theft, arson and resist arrest, you choose the most serious topic and inquire about it only. If unsure, look at the sentencing guidelines of each act to choose the one with the longest sentence.

Types of Questions to Avoid

-Leading - This type of question is phrased in such a way that it suggests the desired answer.
The question can generally be answered with a "yes" or "no" and tends to contaminate the information obtained.
For instance: "You said you saw a car; was it a red car?" Or, "Did you see the red car?"
Leading questions are only acceptable as to test or refresh memory.
Did you see a ....
Didn't you see a ....
Didn't you see the...
Wasn't there a ....

-The negatively phrased question that not only suggests that the response is to be "no," but also implies that, "no" is the right answer.
For example, "You don't know his name, do you?" Or, "You didn't see him, did you?" Or, "You don't remember what she looks like, do you?" Or, "You didn't get the license number, did you?"

The negatively phrased question may indicate to victims or witnesses that they do not know the answer and more importantly, they do not have to try very hard to remember the correct information. For the suspect, a negatively phrased question suggests that "no" is the expected answer and thereby may provide an out."
-Compound Questions contain two or more questions asked in rapid succession before the interviewee can respond to the first one.
Also included in this category is the rephrasing of the original question before a response is obtained to the first version.
Many compound questions contain the word "or."
"Did you go alone, or did someone else go with you?"

Compound questions confuse the interviewee and often cause information to be missed or overlooked. In many instances, when faced with multiple questions, the interviewee will answer only the last or, the least threatening, question.
The answers to the other questions are most often lost because the investigator does not remember to ask them again.
For the suspect, compound questions offer an "out." The suspect may weigh the implications of the answers to each question and answer only the

questions that are least incriminating and cause the least amount of stress.
The suspect will use compound questions as an opportunity to conceal information.
Further, they will rely on the fact that most interviewers will not ask those "lost" questions again.

-Complex questions are complicated, not easily understood, and cover more than one topic.
Complex questions tend to confuse and lead to an, "I don't know," or a false answer.
For example, "Based on your prior knowledge of the circumstances leading up to the incident and the reactions of others indicated by their testimony, what would have been the suspect's actions throughout this period?"

-Never use double negative questions
Didn't he have no dinner?
He couldn't barely stand up?
He never said nothing to nobody?
I couldn't barely hear him.
Didn't you stop at the stop sign before entering the intersection?

Often times they will offer resistance to your broad statement of tell me (write down) everything that happened on … .
Keep your responses neutral.

      Q-What exactly do you want me to say?
      A-Everything you are aware of.
      Q-That'll take me all day! (Known as a procedural complaint)
      A-Just put down everything you are aware of.

A note of interest:
When you have a scheduled interview with a subject and the case is serious enough, it can be very effective to conduct surveillance on that subject the day before the interview and get a thorough account of their activities.
During the interview, you can inquire as to the subject's activities the day before as confirmation questions for use as a scale to balance the veracity of his statement.

Active listening using Interrogatories w/confirmation questions.
You said yesterday you went and ran some errands, what exactly did you do?
I went to the grocery store.
What else did you do?
I just went home.
You said you just went home, where else did you go?

Gets all of the facts. Almost all interviewees can tell you more information than they initially recall or admit knowing. Asks questions about every item discussed.

A review of their statement can expand on our questioning which is accomplished by micro-action questioning. Micro-action questioning is a restatement technique by repeating part of their own statement that requires clarification.

To initiate these micro-actions, have them return to just prior in the narrative where a possible omission of information began. Restate word-for-word the information directly preceding the omission; it is important to use the exact language used by the subject.

Then, have the suspect expand on the previous information, ensuring that they identify any additional gaps in time and missing details.

Some interviewers make the mistake of going directly to the areas of greatest interest thus alerting the subject to specific areas of concern. Instead, they should proceed chronologically, beginning with and closing the first area of omission and patiently moving on to the subsequent areas. Use as many questions as is necessary to satisfy the time period.

OPTIONAL - Have them write five reasons why someone in their position would make up a story similar to theirs. They will often give reasons why they could be guilty which can provide theme material.

Under what conditions would you do something like (whatever is being investigated)?

Compare to their answers from the previous question - Please give me five reasons why you think this happened.

Take as many breaks as needed to confer with your team and develop themes, discuss assessment cues, and determine areas that need clarification. If doubt exists about the story, ask BAIT questions of plausible evidence

BAIT Questions Rules

They should be asked once they have committed themselves to the appropriate denial. You must create the possibility that the bait is real. It should be presented in a way that shows the evidence could exist in the near future. It is to present a possible innocent excuse of evidence.

Possible Presumptive/Bait Themes
Eyewitness
Fingerprints
Footprints
Tire tracks
Timeline issues
Co-conspirators testimony
Cell phone records
Surveillance video
DNA evidence

"Jose, you told us that you left the library at two o'clock and later walked past the library at five o'clock. Now, I'm sure that you are aware that there are surveillance cameras throughout the building. Is there any reason why when we finish viewing all of the security videos that we will see you inside the library at about four o'clock?"

"I am not saying that you were involved in taking the woman's purse, but you know how easy it is to lose track of time. Is it possible that you could be mistaken on the time and were inside the library at around four o'clock?"

Expect protest statements like, "I am not the type of person to do that." or "I'm a devout Christian."
Tell them you are glad to hear that because it reinforces your belief that you were put in this situation.

A truth teller provides you with meaningful, relevant, pertinent, and verifiable information about the crime.

This is a transitional point from the interview to the interrogation.

To assist in this transition employ a technique called "The Hypothetical Approach."
Explain to the suspect that in the beginning, I had an open mind, but after questioning him, I find several issues in his story. I have not drawn any final conclusions, but I want to talk to him on a hypothetical basis.

This transitional argument is:
"Let us assume that you are basically a good person, but that you have become overwhelmed by personal problems."
"You have reached a point in your life where you no longer care, and one more potential embarrassment will not make a difference."
"Suddenly, you view (the money)(issue, etc.) in question as a solution to your immediate problems, and in one impulsive act, you violate a standard of morality that you have used as a guide most of your life."

While talking to the suspect, watch for what are called "buying signals."
Do I have the suspect's attention?
Is he listening intently to what I have to say?
Is he showing no resistance to what I have to say?
Is he nodding his head in agreement?
Does he look more depressed?
Are tears welling-up in his eyes? If so, launch immediately into Accusatory Interrogation.
"You're a nice person, but I know you stole the money."

The subject's reaction to my declaration is the Litmus Test. If there is not a strong denial, I know I am on the right track.

The Mechanics of Questioning

Questions are the principle tools of interviewing. The word question has two meanings:
That which is asked
The act of asking

Good Questions are:
Short and confined to one topic
Make it clear to easily understand
Avoid harsh words

Precise questions help bring out precise answers to keep the discussion moving toward a particular goal.

Good questions should be precise. The following are precise questions in progressive order:

What did you do?
What did you do when you were growing up?
What did you do last year?
What did you do yesterday?
What did you do yesterday afternoon?
What did you do about 1:00 P.M. yesterday?

Seven W's or the interrogatories

What? (What happened?)
When? (When did it happen?)
Where? (Where did it happen?)
Why? (Why did it happen?)

How? (How did it happen?)
Who? (Who was involved?)
Which? (Which one did it?)

The questions "Why" and Why not?" are two of the most powerful questions.

These are the basis of all investigations and to answer each allows a thorough understanding of the events.

Question Sequence

In I&I your goal is resolving questionable issues. As a rule, a sequence of questions is required to resolve each issue, occurrence, situation, or object, in an investigation that needs an explanation.

General to specific sequence:

This is the most efficient method of solving an issue. Seek general information on the setting of the event before exploring details. Place the subject at the scene before inquiring about his acts there. Determine the act before exploring how or why it was done.

Example after a robbery, it was determined that the group divided the money. The next issue to probe is who shared and how much did each receive?

How was the money divided?
At a meeting.

Where did this meeting take place?
In Joes garage.

Do you know Joe's address?
No, I can take you there.

How many people were there?
Five.

Who were they?
Joe, Sam, Pete, myself and Bob.

How was the dividing determined?
Joe split the money into five piles.

How much did each of you receive?
I don't know-Joe placed it in piles in front of us so we didn't stay there too long.

Did you all get the same size pile?
No Joe's was larger because he is in charge.

Do you know how much was in your pile?
Yes.

How do you the amount?
I went to my house and counted it. It was $155.00.

So everyone received about the same amount except Joe who took more?
I guess so.

In this example, the location was determined first, the participants were then identified, the method of dividing was determined, and the approximate amount can be ascertained.

Restatement Questions

Start with known issues and work toward unknowns in each sequence.

You said earlier that you went to Tampa. What means of transportation did you use?
A car.
You said you went in a car. Who's car is it?
My girlfriend Ann.
You drove your girlfriends car to Tampa. Was anyone with you?
Yeah, my friend Steve and John.

And the sequencing continues until all of the questions are answered.

Change of Reference Point

Rarely are you given an exact measurement, time, and space. To assist these efforts try to change the reference point.

How far away was the guy when you first saw him?
He was a ways.
Would you say he was further than that tower over there?
No not that far.
How about the building over there?
A little further than that.
How much more than the building?
Not much.
So if 1000 feet was just past the building you can say about 1000 feet?
Yes.

How tall was the man?
He was very tall.
Was he taller than me?
A little.
How much taller?
About 2-3 inches.

Controlled-answer questions
These types are to stimulate a desired answer.
To stimulate a person to admit he has information.

"I understand you were at the store when the
robbery occurred, describe what happened."
This is stronger than to ask,
"Where you at the store when the robbery
occurred?"

The Three Principle Procedures for Applying Questioning Techniques

Free Narrative – Described earlier. They are to
convey all choosing where to start and where to
end.
Direct Examination – This technique brings out
additional details not mentioned in the free recall.
Begin by asking questions not likely to cause anger.
Ask the questions in an order of sequence.
Ask only one question at a time.
Ask straightforward and clear questions.
Give them enough time to answer.
Repeat or rephrase questions if necessary.
Give them a chance to qualify their answers.
Get all of the facts. They can always tell you more.
After the narrative account, ask questions about
every event. Upon conclusion, ask them to give you

a summary accounting or provide one and ask for corrections.

Use **Cross-Examination** of the testimony to find holes, conflicts, falsehoods, or suspicious actions. Have them repeat information about an event several times. You can do this by asking about it in a different manner. Attempt to keep expanding on details at random. Ask what happened, why it happened, when it happened, who was there, why they were there, how did they come to be there, and what preceded or followed the event.
Then occasionally insinuate a different relationship of detail like; "When did you first meet Bob?" Second – "Tell me what led up to your first meeting with Bob?" Third – "Did Bob give you any indications of his plans prior to the previously mentioned meeting?" Fourth – "How long after the plan with Bob did you learn of the meeting place?"

It is all right to use suggestive questions during cross-examination. "You saw Bob strike the store clerk, did you not?" "Wouldn't you say that only an expert could manipulate the books like that?"

Ask about unknown information as if it was known and about known information as if it were unknown to test them.

Specifically explore areas of vague testimony. Point out problematic issues. It is usually best to ask subjects all questions that stimulate deception before confronting them with the issues. Ask them to explain any and all conflicts in his statement. Any corrected information should also be placed under the same scrutiny as the original.

46

Point out when their testimony does not match with the evidence. Also tell them how their nonverbal's are indicating anxiety. Why? Rationalize with them about their statements. Ask them to imagine that they were an investigator, judge, or jury. How do they expect anyone to accept their story?

Do not point out any lies as they occur. Allow them to build many of them to confront them with all at once later. To point it out early gives them the ability to adjust. Use the free narrative, direct examination and the cross-examination techniques.

For a stolen car, you can ask:

What is the description of the car?
When did this theft take place?
What is the identity of the last driver?
Why was he at this place?
How did the theft occur?
What precautions were taken to prevent the theft?
Who else has knowledge of the theft?
How, when, and to whom was the theft reported?
Who can verify any part of the story?
Who do you suspect of committing the crime?
What is the drivers driving record, arrest record, and current employment?
Was any property of value in the car at the time of the theft?
What else does the driver know of significance?

Firmness is not arrogance, its confidence. These attacks are usually out of fear that you will discover the truth.

<u>FYI Sight and Memory Studies</u>

Visual limitation studies

A well-known person in good lighting can be recognized as far as 150 feet away.
If a person has some physical handicap, dress, or mannerism, they can recognized up to 300 feet.
An unknown person cannot be recognized more than 100 feet.
In bright moonlight, recognition is usually limited to 30 feet.

Memory

When two things have been observed together, a subsequent remembrance of one will bring back the other.
Frequency equates to memory.
Memory decreases with time.
Person will remember the first contact with persons or things better than succeeding events. Be suspicious of the witness who can remember complete details of an event but cannot remember when, why, or how it all transpired.
Incidents that stimulate a strong emotion are easily remembered but lack detail recall.

<u>Handling unfriendly witnesses</u>

Since they will not volunteer information, we have to try to get them to.
Start by asking them unrelated questions to get them talking.
Ask for cooperation with leading questions that are positive and convey their desire to help.

"You want the truth to be known, don't you?"
"If you had any knowledge in this matter, you would naturally want justice, wouldn't you?"
"Then I'm sure you wouldn't mind discussing this with me, do you?"
"You would expect others to help you if you were the victim, wouldn't you?"

If at any point he starts not cooperating again, move the talk back to a topic he cooperated with.

During stiff resistance, at a critical point in an interview, where they are showing defensive attitudes say, "Wait a minute. Please repeat that. I'm not sure I heard you correctly."
This immediately forces them to stop their defenses and focus to that point in question, often to see how they blundered.
The classic accusatorial excuse – "Are you accusing me?" is handled by saying, "I don't know whether you are or are not involved. I am in possession of the facts that will clear those not involved and convict those involved. Let's hear what you have to say."

No factor is too small to receive attention. The ability to reason decreases as the emotions increase. Adjust your questioning speed to the conditions.
Establish a friendly atmosphere, but never allow any doubt about your competence and control of the interrogation.

Whenever a person raises his right hand and invokes religion, pay attention to the exact verbiage that follows. It is here that they will present their first line of defense and it is usually directed to the specific area of stress that bothers him most.

Interrogating subjects of questionable guilt

Assume a neutral position to avoid bias either for or against the subject. Use free narrative, direct examination, and cross-examination to the max by asking as many questions as is possible and avoid showing any reactions to the answers.

When you have finished your questioning and concluded that the person is lying, you have to make the most critical transition in the interrogation: The transition from Non-Accusatory Interviewing to Accusatory Interrogation.

Transitional Accusatory Interrogation

This is an exciting phase of the process because it is moving towards an interrogation and is the first time you are letting the subject know that you believe they are involved. The questions will fall between "Concern" to "Guilt."
Their response will confirm your confidence that you are on the right track.

Transitional questions of concern

"You seem to be thinking about something."
"Something is clearly on your mind."
"Something seems to be bothering you when we talk about ..."
"You seem uncertain when you say..."

Transitional questions of guilt

"Our investigation clearly shows that ..."
"Our investigation indicates you were involved in some way."

Theme developments are based on their reactions. There are several basic requirements to outline for developing interrogational arguments.

Creating Accusatory Arguments

Any argument you employ to break down a suspect's resistance must be based on an underlying truth. If the suspect gets the impression you're lying to him, he will lose respect for you and you lose credibility. Do not insult the intelligence of the suspect. The argument should appeal to his common sense.

The argument should offer a realistic solution to his predicament. Do not dictate to the suspect. Many suspects believe that they lose their manliness by confessing. Indicate to the suspect that he is the captain of his own ship, and you can only offer food for thought.

The decision to tell the truth has to come from him. You have to point out that this is the last time he will have control of his destiny.
If he walks out of your office without telling the truth, the judicial system will dictate his fate.

Any argument you employ should show insight on your part regarding the subject's personality, and the best solution for his problem. Tell a suspect why he committed the crime and why he is not confessing. This tactic seems to take the resistance out of him. You humanize his pain and concern and this understanding helps him talk.

To avoid giving the impression that the suspect is just another number, you have to indicate that you have a personal interest in him. You have to point out that you know that the suspect is capable of telling the truth.
Some of your arguments should have an emotional appeal.

"Your life is not over, there is always hope. This is a new beginning."
"You're not a bad person, you just made a mistake."
"You don't measure a person by a singular act; you have to consider his total existence."
"You measure a person by what he can rise to and not by what he can sink to."
"By telling the truth, you will walk out of this office a lot smarter than when you came in and you will also feel better."

Suspects generally lie out of self-preservation, but they also believe that by lying and denying the crime, they are doing the smart thing. You have to create arguments to show he is not doing the smart thing by denying the crime. Explain that there are too many loopholes in his story.

By lying, he is making a bad situation worse.
He is thinking emotionally rather than rationally.
No jury or judge will believe his story and as it is now he will only insult their intelligence.

"What happened is bad enough, why should he also look like a liar?"
You should point out to the suspect that even a professional criminal knows when to throw in the towel.
There is just too much evidence for the suspect to lie about.

Don't demean him like he's some kind of animal in your arguments. Remember, he has to go on living with himself.
Do not invoke additional guilt feelings.
Always minimize the crime.

Find an attribute of the suspect that you like, and then argue that he could not possess that characteristic and be a liar, too.
Do not give the suspect the impression that you look down on him by personalizing the interrogation.
He will not give you the satisfaction of hearing him confess.
Create arguments that appeal to the self-interest of the suspect.
Do not assume that most people confess because of a stricken conscience.
Most people confess to better their position.
One can live with guilt, which is a private thing.

What most suspects fear is the shame that accompanies the public admission of the crime. You have to help them cope with that shame by pointing out the benefits of gaining personal and public respect through a confession.

Point out to the suspect that to gain self-respect, there are only three things that he can do:

Tell the truth, be sorry for what he did, and get on with his life.
Point out that you cannot gain public respect by insulting people's intelligence.
People may not condone his act but they will respect him for having told the truth.

There are two types of offenders, emotional and non-emotional
Emotional offenders are first time offenders or an employee who takes from the job.
Emotional offenders respond best with theme approaches of family issues and trust, impulsive behaviors, losing control and helping the family. This has the effect of normalizing the criminal behavior of the suspect and, combined with the comfort from the interrogator's apparent sympathy with the suspect, makes it easier for the latter to confess.

A non-emotional is the regular offender with a past criminal history.
Non-emotional offenders are best approached with issues of evidence themes.
He is the one who would break into the office to steal.

The Confession Formula

Even with the use of convincing arguments, some suspects will not confess. This is often attributable to you not being assertive enough. To deal with this a formula is used which is:

Leverage plus the force of the assertion of guilt equals confession.

You, the interviewer with an effective technique, above all else is the main reason why people confess. You learn that you do not obtain confessions simply by asking questions. You do not obtain confessions through the process of cross-examination that is designed to embarrass or discredit the suspect.

You do not obtain confessions by listening to a suspect's story like a human tape recorder. Confessions are obtained by an interrogator who uses arguments to convince the suspect to tell the truth.

These persuasive arguments are called themes. It's not what you say, but how you say it. Good interrogators develop a list of arguments from those used successfully in past cases. During an interrogation, you can draw from the list you believe will convince the subject that he will be better off by telling the truth based on the case analysis and interview.

The demeanor of the interrogator is a key factor. You have to extract the statement legally, which can be difficult in the sense that whatever you say is going to be construed by someone as either a threat or a promise. In any event, to be successful, the confession formula has to be utilized.

Leverage plus the force of the assertion of guilt, equals confession.

Leverage in any interrogation session, is the weight and the amount of evidence you have with which to confront the suspect. Irrefutable evidence creates the ultimate leverage in any interrogation session.

Confronting a suspect with the evidence you have is considered the first level of confrontation.
If the interrogator is not successful at the first level then the second level, which involves the employment of persuasive arguments.
Most confessions come at the second level of confrontation.
With difficult subjects, it is necessary to reach the third level of confrontation that requires an increase in the force of the assertion of guilt.

Thus, <u>the second part of the confession formula:</u>

The force of the assertion of guilt. Successful interrogations demonstrate how strong the assertion of guilt has to be to obtain a confession from most people. The suspect, although guilty, always lives in hope of outlasting the interrogator.

Generally, the suspect will not confess until he is convinced that the interrogator has no doubt as to his guilt and is not going to give up. The interrogator has to give the impression that the issue of guilt or innocence is no longer debatable. The only remaining question is whether or not the suspect has the fortitude to tell the truth.

In most instances, failure to obtain a confession is caused by a lack of evidence with which to confront the suspect or the fact that you are not assertive enough.
A sudden elevation in confidence is the best tactic to employ to obtain a confession.

This is done with a no-nonsense, businesslike approach so the suspect gets the impression you are not giving up.

You can enhance the force of the assertion of guilt by changing body positions. This is done by leaning forward if in a sitting position or by suddenly standing up if seated. The secret to successful interrogation is to create what I call compassionate dominance.

This dominance is created not by physical intimidation or arrogance, but by insightful arguments amplified by the positive assertive demeanor of the interrogator.
Assertive verbalization done in a businesslike manner remarkably increases your probability of obtaining a confession.

Confronting the suspect with the evidence against him, plus the employment of interrogative arguments is not always enough. There has to be a continual build-up in the force of the assertion of guilt. The ultimate assertion of guilt occurs in the interrogation Closure.

Other reasons why suspects confess:

Torture - Worldwide, more confessions are obtained by torture than by any other means.

Psychological Duress - Long periods of continuous interrogation will wear down a suspect's resistance to a point where he will eventually confess simply to get the interrogators off his back which can lead to obtaining a false confession.

The Self-Interest Factor - Man is basically a pain-avoiding, pleasure-seeking animal.
The suspect will always operate from the self-interest principle.
A suspect confesses to ingratiate himself with the interrogator hoping to obtain a lesser penalty.

Resignation: The suspect confesses because there is too much evidence against him and lying would make a bad situation worse.

The Conditioned Response - A conditioning of the person through parental teaching, school, church and state.
This process creates the thing we call conscience.
A violation of principles learned, results in the feeling we call guilt.
Many people can live with guilt by the employment of defense mechanisms.
Others are prompted to confess to decrease guilt feelings.
The person confesses to punish himself.
The confession is a restoration factor; the person confesses to regain personal respect and public acceptance.
The suspect reaches a point where he thinks, "Why be a liar on top of what I already did?"

The Captive Audience Syndrome - The suspect feeds on the personal attention and recognition he gets from the interrogator.
An interrogation creates a strange, symbiotic interpersonal relationship between the suspect and the interrogator.
Many people confess to the act of murder simply to reward the interrogator.

The Vicarious Factor - A confession can recreate the sensual experience that existed at the time of the crime.
The confession allows the suspect to relive the crime. By describing it aloud to the interrogator, the sensual experience is heightened.

The suspect in many instances is prompted to go into the gory details of the crime simply by watching the reactions of the interrogator as he is confessing. Many suspects like to shock the interrogator.

Revenge - Many suspects confess to get revenge against another.

Recognition - Some people confess to gain notoriety for the crime in question.
This factor is the motivation for many unstable people who confess to crimes they do not actually commit.
Guilty people who are motivated by recognition confess to enjoy celebrity status or their brief "moment in the spotlight."

The Institutionalized Suspect - Many ex-convicts are not intimidated or deterred by the possibility of going back to prison.
They do not like the responsibility of freedom.
In some respects, they are happier inside prison than out.
Obtaining a confession from an institutionalized suspect is a lot easier than getting one from a suspect who has an intense fear of going to prison.

RPM Influence

Experienced investigators know that everyone uses an often-unconscious mental process to justify their behavior or cope with personal problems. Criminals frequently employ these defense mechanisms to rationalize their actions, to project blame onto someone or something else, and to minimize their crimes.

While offenders do not reveal these devices, they give clues when investigators ask them about their backgrounds, attitudes, beliefs, and values during the initial interview. The three commonly used defense mechanisms are Rationalization, Projection, and Minimization or RPM's.

By understanding suspects' situations, motivations, and pressures in their lives, investigators can offer possible solutions.

Rationalization offers plausible explanations for suspects' actions that reflect favorably on them. They will rationalize their actions to excuse errors of all kinds and degrees. Come up with an excuse or reason for everything to allow them to save face.

"Everyone's taken something from their work. Cops take things from work. You're not the first person to do something like this."

Projection excuses an act by placing the blame on something or someone else. It expresses that the action is not totally their fault.

Minimizing the offense helps suspects reduce, to their psychological satisfaction, their roles in or the seriousness of their crimes.

By carefully using such soft words as "mistake" and "accident," which minimize the gravity of the situation, investigators can decrease suspects' resistance to persuasion. Convey to them that "nothing is as bad as it seems. It could be worse. We can get through this."   Or
"Using something without permission just isn't that big of a deal. It's like borrowing without permission."

Other ideas to consider:
Socialize – Let them know that this could have happened to anyone. Humans err.
Truth focus - keep them focused not on their actions, but explain this is a fixable problem, but the repairs cannot begin until the truth is told.
"You were going to pay this back weren't you."

To induce a confession, you will need a reserve of face-saving phrases to rationalize actions ("I understand how you might..."), to project the blame onto someone else ("teenagers can be difficult to deal with..."), to minimize the crime ("accidents like this happen..."), and to provide reasons to confess ("only you can tell your side of the story...").

Common Confession Fears

Recognize their fears and formulate a not so bad alternative.

Fear of punishment is a major cause of concern. You explain:

"Whoever decides their punishment has a lot of discretion to use."
"It could be anywhere from a fine, probation to jail depending on the judge."
"The primary determinate in the decision is whether or not you take responsibility for your actions."
However, avoid insinuating a promise.

Reputation – fear of the media coverage –
"The American public has a profound capacity to forgive and forget. There could be some early mentions heard by some, but only until it becomes a full drag out court case does regular continuing coverage take place."

I will be fired –
"Your company was concerned enough to find out what happened and not out and fire you. Maybe their punishment will not be harsh."

Rejection –
"Admitting wrong is the starting point of rebuilding."

Embarrassment –
"Family is always family. Real friends will stand by their friends, wouldn't you?"

Fear of the Snitch label –
Tell them that admitting to their part in a crime is not being a snitch.
Remind him that the co-conspirators will not hesitate to tell-all on him and even blame him for their actions.

Fear of Retaliation –
Remind him that rarely do co-conspirators become a threat because his full confession will cause them to be taken into custody and they will be too concerned with their own defense.
Once in custody they will be trying to blame him for all, so his confession must be complete.

Confession inhibiting factors:
Remorseful
Desire for sympathy
Pride
These are approached as guilt reduction issues.
He has to live with this issue for the rest of his life and only the truth can begin the healing process.

Be empathetic. Encourage him to talk to you about all of the problems and stress he's experiencing.
Let him know that it takes 'guts' to move forward with this.
"A real man stands up and admits his deeds."

Themes

If they continue with protest or convincing statements or get angry, stay calm.
Agree with them with whatever their protest is with empathetic statements and return to the transition.
"You're right. The world is not fair and no one is judging you. That's why it is so important that we resolve this. We just want to fix this so we can all move forward. You want that, right?"
"You seem very bothered and there is only one way to fix that."

In response to the question, "Our investigation indicates that you are involved" and they respond with silence or lack certainty. The weak veracity of the statement is indicative that there is something that bothers him.

The themes will work only if the subject is listening. The subject quiet's and listens
Physical signs of surrender begin to appear.
Themes are shortened and lead towards alternatives.
Establishment of eye contact is important.
Tears at this point indicate subject's guilt.

You're talking to them now so they cannot commit to a lie. Make sure that the sentence following the transition statement is empathetic towards them and always reward them with a positive statement when they agree.
If they offer a weak denial, give them alternative ideas to lessen the stress.
Bad situation v. good. (Choice Questions)
A statement criticizing the bad reason and a statement praising the positive.
If no response, change themes. The choice question helps to answer why they committed the crime.

It should contain both a statement criticizing the bad reason and a statement praising the positive. A leading question to accept the good reason. A follow up statement after the initial statement was made.

"Listen to me John. Things happen that we can't control. These types of things happen all the time. You're not the only person to have this happen to.

We need the truth and sometimes the truth is difficult and still together we can move through this and make it start to get better. I'd like to think you'd want that too. Right?"

Criticizing the bad – "John, you don't seem to be the type who would do something like this for drugs. If you are then no one is going to believe you."
Praising the good – "John, if you took the money to do something for your family, then that is something everyone would understand. Everyone knows anyone would do anything for their family."
Choice question – "John, did you take that money to buy drugs or to help your family."

The idea here is to create an environment in which they want to give up the truth. We are now implying that we know what they've done and you UNDERSTAND the pressures that led to their ERROR of JUDGEMENT, and if they will take you into their confidence the entire MISUNDERSTANDING can get fixed.

Common reasons for crime occurrences

Education
Parental Relations
Peer Influence
Substance Abuse

Presumptive ideas for questioning and themes

* Murder/Assaults/Rape are violent crimes that often occur on impulse when emotions run high. Alcohol or drug use by the attacker is behind 30 to 50 percent of violent crime.

Anger, jealously, revenge, or pride.

* Property crimes like robberies, burglaries, and auto thefts are usually planned in advance.
"Were you tricked into this?"
"Was it simply an opportunity because careless people left their car unlocked?"
"Peer pressure?"
"Helping your family because of job loss?"
"Bullying in school to prove something?"

Common Choice Questions

Did you steal the money to pay for your habits or did you need money to feed your family? It was to feed your family, wasn't it.
Did you intend to do this or was it just an accident? It was an accident, wasn't it.
Has this happened before or was this the first time because things have been really tough? It was the first time due to rough times wasn't it.
Did you plan this or did it just happen?
Did you commit all of the burglaries in this area or just this one?
Have you done this several times or just this once?
Was this your plan or were you being pushed by the others?
Did you start this or did she come on to you?
Were you going to sell those drugs or was it only for your personal use?
Was this your idea or someone else's?
Did you search the house for money or was it just laying around?
Did you intend to hurt her or was it something that just happened?

Did you intend to keep the money or were you going to pay it back?
Were you going to use the drugs while you were at work or after you were off and away from the job?
Was the car door locked or was the doors left open?

If appropriate, ask them as a sign of good faith if they would be willing to compensate the victim for their loss.
If they confess, even a little, reward them with praise and empathy.
Let them know how strong they are to tell the truth.
"Let's fix this with the truth because that is the only way. I'd like to think you would want to that, right?"
If they agree to the lesser reason and the evidence indicates otherwise, you must move the confession to the real reason.
If they say they did neither, restate the accusation and present the same or new choices.

Follow up questions should be general in nature and encourage the subject to keep talking:
"Tell me more about that?"
"What happened next?"
"When did you begin having sexual relations with …?"
"When did you first get the idea to take the money?"
"Tell me your side of the story."
"Tell me about the last time you lost your temper with your child."

Be patient. Most will confess to only a small amount of info and the rest has to be brought out. If they confess, keep working the story and try to get the real reasons that fit with the evidence. If everything points to them, use accusatorial questions.

Closure is the concluding section of your argument. A weak closure negates even the most effective interrogative arguments.
Closure is the culmination in one statement of the force of the assertion of guilt,
"You did kill her, didn't you?"

CLOSURE

Confessions are obtained by persuasive interrogational arguments, the employment of the confession formula, and closure.
Of the three, closure is the most difficult for many interrogators. In fact, it is the most difficult part of any sales effort. Fear of failure causes weak and tentative closure.

The interrogator hoping for a confession, yet fearful the suspect will not acknowledge guilt puts off closure. Good closure is a matter of timing. Sometimes closure is premature.

Other times it is so late that the interrogator talks the suspect right out of confessing. Professional sales people call this "talking past the sale."
I have observed many interrogations, and quite often, I have said to myself, "When is he ever going to ask the suspect if he did it?"

You have to sense when to close. You get a feeling when the suspect is ready to confess. An ambivalent suspect, wavering in his decision as to whether or not to confess, will succumb to a forceful no-nonsense closure.

There are several types of closure.
Choose the type that fits the mental toughness of the suspect. With weak suspects, you can use the direct approach:
"You did steal that money didn't you?"

It is easier for a suspect to confess to a detail of a crime than to make a sudden full disclosure.
Therefore, try a forceful, but softer approach.
"You still have some of that money left, don't you?"
           Or
"You can take me to the gun you used, can't you?"
If the suspect replies in the affirmative, it's obvious that you are going to get a full confession.

The third type of closure involves giving the suspect a nice reason for committing the act rather than the real reason. For example:
"If you had time to think you probably would not have done it."
"I get the impression that this was just an impulsive thing on your part, isn't that true?"
"You seem like a nice person to me, and I don't think you would have stolen this money if you weren't going crazy because of unpaid bills, isn't that true?"
Preface closure with a compliment, because friendliness begets friendliness.
I will pick out some characteristics of the suspect, and use it to assist closure.
"I have talked to you long enough to know that you are basically a good person and not a liar. You did take that money, didn't you?"

If you acknowledge the good parts of his character, he is more apt to admit the bad parts. Do not show disappointment on your face if the suspect does not confess.

Without missing a beat, reiterate some of your interrogational arguments and close again. Success is predicated on patience and perseverance.

Accusatorial or Relevant Questions

Keep them simple and direct. We are trying to get them to confess to any of the information. Along this line, ask soft words:

Needed vs stole

Fudged the books vs embezzlement

Avoid using legal jargon and other words that may be perceived as being emotion evoking or judgmental.

AVOID: Assault, Rape, Sodomize, Murder, Molest, Mutilate

Accusatorial or Relevant Questions

(Accuse) "You took" (not stole) or (Relevant) "Did you take (not steal) any of the missing money?"

"You were" or "Were you involved in any way with the loss (not theft) of the missing money?"

Did you shoot the victim or by name? Were you involved in any way with shooting the victim?

Ask only one action in one question, "Did you break into the victims house or (name's) house?" "Did you know the house was going to be broken into?"

Maintain a level mode and tone. If they respond in an evasive manner, return to your discussion of fixing the problem.

If they give you an emphatic "no," ask a BAI

"Why should I believe you?"

The only acceptable answer is some derivation of, "Because I'm telling you the truth."

Try to imagine yourselves in the suspect's position in order to understand their motivation for becoming involved.
For example: During the break-in and theft of money, the motive of the suspect is more likely the theft of money, and not the break-in.
Therefore, the target of your relevant questions would be the theft.
Consider the case facts when selecting the target for relevant questions. You should target the area that connects the suspect most closely to the crime. This connection can often be identified by case facts, circumstantial evidence, or other information contained in the investigative file.

You may never get the entire story. Know the elements of the crime you are investigating. Start with the easiest elements such as opportunity and then work towards the crime itself. Get all of the facts you can and understand that there will always be more.

Try to get an apology letter from them to whomever and if agreed, leave them alone to do it.

Say to the subject, "I'm going to give you an opportunity that I give everyone and they've all agreed." Socializing persuasion

Closing – I want to thank you for your time today. If I have any other questions, you would agree to talk to me again, wouldn't you? If they do not - I don't understand. When we spoke before, you agreed

that you would talk with me again. Why are you now unable to do so? What's changed?
Tell the subject that they will remember additional information and ask them to please write it down and call you as soon as practical.

No matter how the interview goes, end it as professionally as you started to give them a better feeling about talking to you in the future. They may say "no" to each of the questions, but you will have to use your information obtained that shows all of the deception points in their statement and combined with the physical evidence of the case to make the determination to charge.

I&I Checklist

Case Analysis

Case Reports

Previous Case Reports

Field Interview Reports

Witness Interviews

Evidence

    Potential BAIT Themes

Photos

Name

Address

DOB

Motive

Develop several Comparison and BAI

questions

Non-Accusatory Approach or Accusatory

Elements of the crime

Why do you need to interview the subject

What are the unknowns

Multiple interviews – Order of Interviews

Prepare the Interview Room

Verify the audio-video equipment

Water and/or snack

Do Not Disturb Signal

Confirm the need for a restroom break

Conduct a physical search

Look and dress appropriate

Introduction

Intro you and them

Show credentials

Introduce others

Purpose Confirmation

Physical Assessment

Background

Attitude questions establishing baselines

"Tell me about yourself."

Use bio for confirmation and pay attention to the detail

Have you been previously questioned but not arrested in any other matter?

Are they cooperating?

Do they appear to have the propensity to have committed the crime?

Employment and history

Watch for a possible catalyst in their behavior for the crime of investigation

Honesty or Lie test

Before we start, how do you think this investigation will turn out for you?

The Interview

The Witness Interview page

Witness statement example

Question chronologically

What initiated the events

Explore incidental information that was
happening around them at the time

Ask verification questions

Determine if the story is logical

Look for vague answers

Beware of the person who has a singular
excuse

Are there realistic feelings

Projection of blame to others

When they focus on not being involved, focus
on their alibi

What were their actions after the event

Ask an all-inclusive question, anything known,
not asked about?

TEDS stands for:

"Tell me..."

"Explain to me..."

"Describe for me..."

"Show me...."

PIE stands for:

"Precisely..."

"In detail..."

"Exactly...."

Focus on the 7 W's

What? (What happened?)

When? (When did it happen?)

Where? (Where did it happen?)

Why? (Why did it happen?)

How? (How did it happen?)

Who? (Who was involved?)

Which? (Which one did it?)

Start with the free narrative

Direct Examination

Cross-Examination

The Interrogation

Remember the Confession Formula - Leverage plus the force of the assertion of guilt equals confession

Develop Rationalizations, Projections, and Minimizations

Have your choice questions ready based on evidence, statements, and attitude

When all points to them, move to your accusatorial statements

Ask them for a letter of apology

Have a professional closing no matter which way it goes

Bibliography

Adams, Susan H., Napier, Michael R. (October 1995). Magic Words to Obtain Confessions, FBI Law Enforcement Bulletin

FIFRA Interviewing Tecniques, Appendix B, B-1 through B-28.

Holmes, Warren D. (1995) Polygraph, Volume 24, Number 4; American Polygraph Association

Royal, Robert F., Schutt, Steven R. (1976)The Gentle Art of Interviewing and Interrogation; Prentice-Hall, Inc.

Varnell, Steven (2013). "Behavior Analysis and Interviewing Techniques", Steven Varnell Publishing.

About the Author

Steven C Varnell is a based in Apollo Beach, Florida. He has a B.S. degree from the University of West Florida and is a retired Florida State Trooper having served from 1982 – 2011. In 1984, he piloted the State of Florida's Drug Interdiction Program and was involved with Drug and Criminal Investigations for 27 years. He has experience in investigations ranging from fraud and theft to narcotics and homicide.

Steve is a law enforcement-training specialist. As a certified instructor by the Florida Criminal Justice Standards and Training Commission, he taught police topics to his own and numerous other city, county, state, and federal agencies. Steve is a certified Interviews and Interrogations and High Liability instructor. As an adjunct instructor for St Petersburg College, he taught police agencies throughout the country at every level, courses in interdiction, officer safety, patrol, interviews, interrogations, behavior analysis, and written statement analysis.

Steve has received recognition by nearly every federal, local, county, and state law enforcement agencies. He is the only law enforcement officer to receive the Officer of the Year award in Hillsborough County, Florida three separate times for his work in drug investigations. He received a commendation award by the International Narcotic Officers Association, presented at Reno, Nevada in 1993. He is also the recipient of the annual ASIS International Law Enforcement Recognition Award (2006) for his work in narcotics investigations.

Steve is a continuous student in the field of interviewing, interrogations, behavioral recognition, written statement analysis, and officer safety and survival. His persistent research of techniques tested worldwide is the foundation for his ability to present the most practical information available providing the real world knowledge that instruction of this nature demands.

For more information on training, refer to isspolicetraining.com

www.ingramcontent.com/pod-product-compliance
Lightning Source LLC
Chambersburg PA
CBHW060641210326
41520CB00010B/1688